D0598215

soups

simple and delicious easy-to-make recipes

Frances Ros

p

This is a Parragon Publishing Book
First published in 2002

Parragon Publishing
Queen Street House
4 Queen Street
Bath, BA1 1HE, UK

Copyright © Parragon 2002

All rights reserved. No part of this publication
may be reproduced, stored in a retrieval system or
transmitted, in any form or by any means, electronic,
mechanical, photocopying, recording, or otherwise,
without the prior permission of the copyright holder.

ISBN: 0-75258-870-2

Printed in China

Produced by the Bridgewater Book Company Ltd.

Photographer Calvey Taylor-Haw

Home Economist Ruth Pollock

NOTES FOR THE READER

- This book uses both imperial and metric measurements. Follow the same units of measurement throughout; do not mix imperial and metric.

- All spoon measurements are level: teaspoons are assumed to be 5 ml, and tablespoons are assumed to be 15 ml.

- Unless otherwise stated, milk is assumed to be whole milk, eggs and individual vegetables such as potatoes are medium, and pepper is freshly ground black pepper.

- Recipes using raw or very lightly cooked eggs should be avoided by infants, the elderly, pregnant women, convalescents, and anyone suffering from an illness.

- The times given are an approximate guide only. Preparation times differ according to the techniques used by different people and the cooking times may also vary from those given. Optional ingredients, variations, or serving suggestions have not been included in the calculations.

contents

introduction

There is no substitute for good, homemade soup, and creating soups at home can be a tremendously enjoyable experience. You need very little in the way of basic cooking equipment, just a large pan with a lid and a sharp knife for chopping. A large skillet or wok is also helpful, but not essential.

Soup can be very economical to make—you can use leftovers to make some delicious concoctions, from light appetizers and snacks to more substantial soups that are meals in themselves. On special occasions, you can splash out on more expensive ingredients and create impressive soups that will grace any dinner table.

Soups are very nutritious, too, and can be packed with healthy ingredients such as vegetables, fish, beans, and rice. Many are low in fat, and high-fat ingredients such as cream can be replaced with lower fat alternatives.

Soup is also a popular international food. Many of the recipes included in this book reflect the rich diversity of the different cuisines found across the world, so wherever you happen to be—and whatever the occasion—you are bound to find something in its pages to satisfy your taste and delight your dinner guests.

guide to recipe key		
	very easy	Recipes are graded as follows: 1 pea = easy; 2 peas = very easy; 3 peas = extremely easy.
	serves 4	Recipes generally serve four people. Simply halve the ingredients to serve two, taking care not to mix imperial and metric measurements.
	10 minutes	Preparation time. Where marinating, chilling, or cooling are involved, these times have been added on separately: eg, 15 minutes + 30 minutes to marinate.
	10 minutes	Cooking time. Cooking times do not include the cooking of side dishes or accompaniments served with the main dishes.

mushroom & sherry soup
page 18

bouillabaisse
page 42

sausage & red cabbage soup
page 70

spicy lentil soup
page 76

vegetable soups

Vegetables are very healthy foods and make nutritious, satisfying ingredients in soups. The combinations of texture and flavor in this section are endless. From the chilled Gazpacho, with its ripe tomatoes and red bell peppers, to the delightful Vegetable Soup with Pesto, packed with fresh basil and garlic, there are mouthwatering recipes for every season using every type of vegetable. Alcohol is also a great favorite in soups, so why not try the Mushroom & Sherry Soup? And for cheese lovers, the Sweet Potato & Stilton Soup cannot be missed.

gazpacho

		ingredients	
extremely easy	1 lb 2 oz/500 g large ripe tomatoes 4 tbsp extra-virgin olive oil	GARNISH croûtons (see page 24)	
serves 4	3 scallions, trimmed and chopped 2 red bell peppers, seeded and chopped	sprigs of fresh basil fresh crusty rolls, to serve	
15 minutes + 2–3 hours to chill	3 garlic cloves, chopped 1 cucumber, peeled and chopped 1 tbsp red wine vinegar 1 tbsp chopped mixed herbs salt and pepper		
—			

First, skin the tomatoes. Bring a pot of water to a boil, put the tomatoes into a heatproof bowl, then pour over enough boiling water to cover them. Let soak for about 3 minutes, then lift the tomatoes out of the water and let cool slightly. When they are cool enough to handle, gently pierce the skins with the point of a knife. Remove and discard the skins.

Cut the tomatoes in half and remove the seeds. Chop the flesh and put it into a food processor. Add the oil, scallions, bell peppers, garlic, cucumber, vinegar, and mixed herbs to the food processor. Season with salt and pepper and blend until smooth. Push the blended mixture through a strainer into a large bowl, then cover with plastic wrap and refrigerate for 2–3 hours.

Ladle the chilled soup into serving bowls and garnish with croûtons and sprigs of fresh basil. Serve with fresh crusty rolls.

vichyssoise

		ingredients	
very easy			
serves 4	2 tbsp butter 2 shallots, chopped 2 large leeks, trimmed and sliced 1 lb/450 g potatoes, peeled and diced 1 tbsp chopped fresh chives 1 bay leaf 2½ cups vegetable bouillon salt and pepper ½ cup light cream	GARNISH swirl of light cream chopped fresh chives fresh crusty rolls, to serve	
15–20 minutes + 2¼ hours to cool/chill			
35 minutes			

Melt the butter in a large pan over medium heat. Add the shallots and cook, stirring, for 2 minutes, until slightly softened. Add the leeks and cook, stirring, for another 2 minutes. Add the potatoes, chives, bay leaf, and bouillon, and season with salt and pepper. Bring to a boil, then reduce the heat, cover the pan, and simmer for 30 minutes. Remove from the heat and let the soup cool for 15 minutes.

Remove and discard the bay leaf, then transfer the soup into a food processor and blend until smooth (you may need to do this in batches). Transfer into a large bowl and stir in the cream. Cover with plastic wrap and chill in the refrigerator for at least 2 hours.

When ready to serve, remove from the refrigerator and ladle into serving bowls. Garnish each bowl with a swirl of cream and some chopped fresh chives and serve with fresh crusty rolls.

leek & potato soup

		ingredients	
	very easy	2 tbsp butter	generous ¾ cup crème fraîche or
		2 garlic cloves, chopped	plain yogurt
	serves 4	3 large leeks, trimmed and sliced	3½ oz/100 g smoked firm cheese, such
		1 lb/450 g potatoes, peeled and	as Applewood, grated
		chopped into bite-size chunks	
	15–20 minutes + 10 minutes to cool	1 tbsp chopped fresh parsley	GARNISH
		1 tbsp chopped fresh oregano	chopped fresh parsley
		1 bay leaf	fresh chives
		3½ cups vegetable bouillon	thick slices of fresh crusty bread,
	35 minutes	salt and pepper	to serve

Melt the butter in a large pan over medium heat. Add the garlic and cook, stirring, for 1 minute. Add the leeks and cook, stirring, for another 2 minutes. Add the potatoes, herbs, and bouillon, and season with salt and pepper. Bring to a boil, then reduce the heat, cover the pan, and simmer for 25 minutes. Remove from the heat, let cool for 10 minutes, then remove and discard the bay leaf.

Transfer half of the soup into a food processor and blend until smooth (you may need to do this in batches). Return to the pan with the rest of the soup, stir in the crème fraîche, and reheat gently. Season with salt and pepper.

Remove from the heat and stir in the cheese. Ladle into serving bowls and garnish with chopped fresh parsley and chives. Serve with thick slices of fresh crusty bread.

pea & mint soup

		ingredients	
very easy	1 tbsp butter	sprigs of fresh mint, to garnish	
	3 shallots, chopped	slices of fresh whole-wheat bread, to serve	
serves 4	2 leeks, trimmed and finely chopped		
	1 potato, peeled and chopped		
	1 lb/450 g frozen peas		
15 minutes + 10 minutes to cool	2 tbsp chopped fresh mint		
	3½ cups vegetable bouillon		
	salt and pepper		
40 minutes			

Melt the butter in a large pan over medium heat. Add the shallots and cook, stirring, for 2 minutes. Add the leeks and cook, stirring, for another 2 minutes. Add the potato, peas, chopped mint, and bouillon, and season with salt and pepper. Bring to a boil, then reduce the heat, cover the pan, and simmer for 30 minutes. Remove from the heat and let cool for 10 minutes.

Transfer the soup into a food processor and blend until smooth (you may need to do this in batches). Return to the pan, season with salt and pepper, and reheat gently.

Remove from the heat and pour into individual serving bowls. Garnish the soup with sprigs of fresh mint and serve with slices of fresh whole-wheat bread.

creamy carrot & parsnip soup

		ingredients	
very easy		4 tbsp butter	GARNISH
		1 large onion, chopped	light cream
serves 4		1 lb/450 g carrots, peeled and chopped	sprigs of fresh cilantro
		2 large parsnips, peeled and chopped	
		1 tbsp grated fresh gingerroot	fresh crusty rolls, to serve
15–20 minutes + 10 minutes to cool		1 tsp grated orange zest	
		2½ cups vegetable bouillon	
		½ cup light cream	
55 minutes–1 hour		salt and pepper	

Melt the butter in a large pan over low heat. Add the onion and cook, stirring, for 3 minutes, until slightly softened. Add the carrots and parsnips, cover the pan, and cook, stirring occasionally, for about 15 minutes, until the vegetables have softened a little. Stir in the gingerroot, orange zest, and bouillon. Bring to a boil, then reduce the heat, cover the pan, and simmer for 30–35 minutes, until the vegetables are tender. Remove the soup from the heat and let cool for 10 minutes.

Transfer the soup into a food processor and blend until smooth (you may need to do this in batches). Return the soup to the pan, stir in the cream, and season well with salt and pepper. Warm through gently over low heat.

Remove from the heat and ladle into soup bowls. Garnish each bowl with a swirl of cream and a sprig of fresh cilantro and serve with fresh crusty rolls.

mushroom & sherry soup

		ingredients	
very easy	4 tbsp butter	3 tbsp all-purpose flour
	2 garlic cloves, chopped	$^1/_2$ cup milk
serves 4	3 onions, sliced	2 tbsp sherry
	1 lb/450 g mixed white and chestnut	$^1/_2$ cup sour cream
	mushrooms, sliced	
15 minutes	3$^1/_2$ oz/100 g fresh cèpes or porcini	GARNISH
	mushrooms, sliced	sour cream
	3 tbsp chopped fresh parsley	chopped fresh parsley
40 minutes	generous 2 cups vegetable bouillon	fresh crusty rolls, to serve
	salt and pepper	

Melt the butter in a large pan over low heat. Add the garlic and onions and cook, stirring, for 3 minutes, until slightly softened. Add the mushrooms and cook for another 5 minutes, stirring. Add the chopped parsley, pour in the bouillon, and season with salt and pepper. Bring to a boil, then reduce the heat, cover the pan, and simmer for 20 minutes.

Put the flour into a bowl, mix in enough milk to make a smooth paste, then stir it into the soup. Cook, stirring, for 5 minutes. Stir in the remaining milk and the sherry and cook for another 5 minutes. Remove from the heat and stir in the sour cream. Return the pan to the heat and warm gently.

Remove from the heat and ladle into serving bowls. Garnish with sour cream and chopped fresh parsley, and serve the soup with crusty rolls.

vegetable soup with pesto

		ingredients	
very easy		2 tbsp olive oil	PESTO
		2 garlic cloves, chopped	2 garlic cloves, chopped
		2 onions, chopped	1 oz/25 g fresh basil leaves
serves 4		1 celery stalk, trimmed and chopped	generous ¾ cup grated Parmesan
		1 carrot, peeled and chopped	cheese
		5 cups vegetable bouillon	5 tbsp extra-virgin olive oil
20 minutes		1 potato, peeled and chopped	generous ¾ cup pine nuts
		6 oz/175 g frozen peas	
		14 oz/400 g canned cannellini beans	sprigs of fresh basil, to garnish
45 minutes		salt and pepper	fresh focaccia, to serve
		1 tbsp chopped fresh basil	

Heat 2 tablespoons of olive oil a large pan over low heat. Add the garlic and onions and cook, stirring, for 3 minutes, until slightly softened. Add the celery and carrot and cook for another 5 minutes, stirring. Pour in the bouillon, then add the potato, peas, and beans. Season with salt and pepper. Bring to a boil, then reduce the heat, cover the pan, and simmer for 30 minutes.

Meanwhile, to make the pesto, put all the ingredients into a food processor and blend until smooth.

Stir the chopped basil into the soup and cook for another 5 minutes. Remove from the heat and ladle into serving bowls. Garnish each bowl with a generous tablespoonful of pesto and a sprig of basil, and serve with fresh focaccia.

asparagus & lemon soup

		ingredients	
very easy	2 tbsp butter	salt and pepper
	3 leeks, trimmed and sliced	1 lb/450 g young, tender asparagus,
serves 4	1 celery stalk, trimmed and sliced	cut into 1-inch/2.5-cm pieces
	5 cups vegetable bouillon	½ cup light cream
	1 tbsp finely grated lemon zest	
15–20 minutes + 10 minutes to cool	2 tbsp lemon juice	fine strips of lemon zest, to garnish
	1 potato, peeled and chopped	fresh crusty rolls, to serve
	1 tbsp chopped fresh parsley	
40 minutes		

Melt the butter in a large pan over medium heat. Add the leeks and cook, stirring, for 3 minutes, until slightly softened. Add the celery and cook for another 3 minutes, stirring. Add the bouillon, lemon zest and juice, potato, and parsley, and season with salt and pepper. Bring to a boil, then reduce the heat, cover the pan, and simmer for 25 minutes. Add the asparagus and cook for another 5 minutes. Remove from the heat and let cool for 10 minutes.

Transfer half of the soup into a food processor and blend until smooth. Return to the pan with the rest of the soup, stir in the cream, and reheat gently.

Remove from the heat and ladle into serving bowls. Garnish with fine strips of lemon zest and serve with fresh crusty rolls.

onion soup with croûtons

		ingredients	
very easy	scant ½ cup butter	CROUTONS
	2 garlic cloves, crushed	2 tbsp olive oil
serves 4	3 large onions, thinly sliced	2 slices day-old white bread,
	1 tsp sugar	crusts removed
	2 tbsp all-purpose flour	
15–20 minutes	scant 1 cup dry white wine	slices of fresh whole-wheat and white
	6¼ cups vegetable bouillon	bread, to serve
	salt and pepper	
1 hour		

Melt the butter in a large pan over medium heat. Add the garlic, onions, and sugar and cook, stirring, for about 25 minutes, until the onions have caramelized.

In a bowl, mix the flour with enough wine to make a smooth paste, then stir it into the onion mixture. Cook for 2 minutes, then stir in the remaining wine and the bouillon. Season with salt and pepper. Bring to a boil, then reduce the heat, cover the pan, and simmer for 30 minutes.

Meanwhile, to make the croûtons, heat the oil in a skillet until hot. Cut the bread into small cubes and cook over high heat, stirring, for about 2 minutes, until crisp and golden. Remove from the heat, drain the croûtons on paper towels, and set them aside.

When the soup is cooked, remove from the heat and ladle into serving bowls. Scatter over some fried croûtons and serve with slices of whole-wheat and white bread.

italian tomato soup

		ingredients	
very easy	2 tbsp extra-virgin olive oil	4 tbsp chopped fresh basil	
	2 large garlic cloves, crushed	4 tbsp mascarpone	
serves 4	1 large onion, chopped 2 lb/900 g ripe vine tomatoes, skinned (see page 8), seeded, and coarsely	sprigs of fresh basil, to garnish	
20 minutes + 10 minutes to cool	chopped, juices reserved generous 1¾ cups vegetable bouillon salt and pepper	TO SERVE small slices of fresh ciabatta thinly sliced mozzarella	
50–55 minutes			

Heat the oil in a large pan over medium heat. Add the garlic and onion and cook, stirring, for about 2 minutes, until slightly softened. Add the tomatoes and their juices and cook for another 3 minutes, then pour in the bouillon and season with salt and pepper. Bring to a boil, then lower the heat, cover the pan, and simmer for about 35–40 minutes. Remove from the heat and let cool for 10 minutes.

Transfer half of the soup into a food processor and blend until smooth. Return to the pan with the rest of the soup, stir in the chopped basil, and cook for another 5 minutes. Stir in the mascarpone and heat through briefly.

Remove from the heat and ladle into serving bowls. Garnish with sprigs of fresh basil and serve with slices of ciabatta topped with thin slices of mozzarella.

sweet potato & stilton soup

		ingredients	
	very easy	4 tbsp butter	pepper
		1 large onion, chopped	$^2/_3$ cup heavy cream
	serves 4	2 leeks, trimmed and sliced	5$^1/_2$ oz/150 g Stilton cheese, crumbled
		6 oz/175 g sweet potatoes, peeled and diced	2 tbsp finely crumbled Stilton cheese, to garnish
	15–20 minutes + 10 minutes to cool	3$^1/_2$ cups vegetable bouillon	
		1 tbsp chopped fresh parsley	thick slices of fresh bread, to serve
		1 bay leaf	
	45 minutes		

Melt the butter in a large pan over medium heat. Add the onion and leeks and cook, stirring, for about 3 minutes, until slightly softened. Add the sweet potatoes and cook for another 5 minutes, stirring, then pour in the bouillon, add the parsley and the bay leaf, and season with pepper. Bring to a boil, then lower the heat, cover the pan, and simmer for about 30 minutes. Remove from the heat and let cool for 10 minutes. Remove and discard the bay leaf.

Transfer half of the soup into a food processor and blend until smooth. Return to the pan with the rest of the soup, stir in the cream, and cook for another 5 minutes. Gradually stir in the crumbled Stilton until melted (do not let the soup boil).

Remove from the heat and ladle into serving bowls. Garnish with finely crumbled Stilton and serve with slices of fresh bread.

seafood soups

Fish and shellfish are very nutritious and quick to cook. Many are low in calories and fat, yet rich in protein and nutrients such as B vitamins. They are also an excellent source of iodine, which helps to maintain a healthy thyroid gland and keeps the metabolism running efficiently. Above all, however, fish and shellfish are delicious, and impart a marvelous richness to soups. Always buy the freshest you can find, and you will be rewarded with soups that are unparalleled in terms of quality and flavor.

traditional salmon soup

		ingredients	
very easy		2 tbsp butter	salt and pepper
		1 onion, chopped	10½ oz/300 g skinless salmon fillets,
serves 4		1 leek, trimmed and sliced	cut into bite-size pieces
		1 tbsp all-purpose flour	2 egg yolks
		generous 2¾ cups fish bouillon	scant ½ cup heavy cream
15 minutes		1 large potato, peeled and chopped	sprigs of fresh dill, to garnish
		1 tbsp chopped fresh parsley	
		1 tbsp chopped fresh dill	slices of crusty bread, to serve
40 minutes			

Melt the butter in a large pan over medium heat. Add the onion and leek and cook, stirring, for 3 minutes, until slightly softened. In a bowl, mix the flour with enough bouillon to make a smooth paste and stir it into the pan. Cook, stirring, for 1 minute, then gradually stir in the remaining bouillon with the potato, parsley, and dill. Season with salt and pepper. Bring to a boil, then lower the heat, cover the pan, and simmer for 25 minutes.

Add the salmon to the pan and cook for about 6 minutes until cooked through. In a clean bowl, whisk together the egg yolks and cream, then stir into the soup.

Remove from the heat and ladle into serving bowls. Garnish with sprigs of fresh dill and serve with slices of crusty bread.

tuna chowder

		ingredients	
	very easy	2 tbsp butter	salt and pepper
		1 large garlic clove, chopped	1 zucchini, trimmed and chopped
	serves 4	1 large onion, sliced	8 oz/225 g canned tuna in
		1 carrot, peeled and chopped	brine, drained
		$2\frac{1}{2}$ cups fish bouillon	1 tbsp chopped fresh basil
	15–20 minutes	14 oz/400 g potatoes, peeled and cut into bite-size chunks	1 tbsp chopped fresh parsley
			scant $\frac{1}{2}$ cup heavy cream
		14 oz/400 g canned chopped tomatoes	sprigs of fresh basil, to garnish
	50 minutes	14 oz/400 g canned cannellini beans, drained	thick slices of whole-wheat bread, to serve
		1 tbsp tomato paste	

Melt the butter in a large pan over low heat. Add the garlic and onion and cook, stirring, for 3 minutes, until slightly softened. Add the carrot and cook for another 5 minutes, stirring. Pour in the bouillon, then add the potatoes, tomatoes, beans, and tomato paste. Season with salt and pepper. Bring to a boil, then reduce the heat, cover the pan, and simmer for 20 minutes.

Add the zucchini, tuna, and chopped basil and parsley and cook for another 15 minutes. Stir in the cream and cook the soup very gently for another 2 minutes.

Remove from the heat and ladle into serving bowls. Garnish with sprigs of fresh basil, and serve with slices of whole-wheat bread.

cullen skink

		ingredients	

![]	very easy	2 tbsp butter
		1 onion, chopped
		1 leek, trimmed and chopped
		2 tbsp all-purpose flour
		3 $\frac{1}{2}$ cups milk
		1 bay leaf
		2 tbsp chopped fresh parsley
		salt and pepper
		12 oz/350 g smoked haddock
		    fillets, skinned
			1 lb/450 g potatoes, peeled, cooked,
			    and mashed
			6 tbsp heavy cream
			
			chopped fresh parsley, to garnish
			
			TO SERVE
			fresh crusty rolls
			fresh salad greens

	serves 4		
	15 minutes		
	40 minutes		

Melt the butter in a large pan over medium heat. Add the onion and leek and cook, stirring, for about 3 minutes, until slightly softened. In a bowl, mix the flour with enough milk to make a smooth paste and stir it into the pan. Cook, stirring, for 2 minutes, then gradually stir in the remaining milk. Add the bay leaf and chopped parsley and season. Bring to a boil, then lower the heat and simmer for 15 minutes.

Rinse the haddock fillets under cold running water, drain, cut into bite-size chunks, and add them to the soup. Cook for 15 minutes, until the fish is tender and cooked right through. Add the mashed potatoes and stir in the cream. Cook for another 2–3 minutes, then remove from the heat and discard the bay leaf.

Ladle into serving bowls, garnish with chopped fresh parsley, and serve with fresh crusty rolls and fresh salad greens.

haddock & shrimp chowder

		ingredients	
very easy	1 tbsp butter	4 ¹/₂ oz/125 g frozen corn
	1 onion, chopped	kernels, thawed
serves 4	3 tbsp all-purpose flour	9 oz/250 g shrimp, cooked and peeled
	generous 2 cups fish bouillon	generous ³/₄ cup heavy cream
	1 bay leaf	
	salt and pepper	whole cooked shrimp, to garnish
20 minutes	generous 2 cups milk	TO SERVE
	2 tbsp dry white wine	fresh whole-wheat bread
	juice and grated zest of 1 lemon	fresh salad greens
40 minutes	1 lb/450 g haddock fillets, skinned	

Melt the butter in a large pan over medium heat. Add the onion and cook, stirring, for about 3 minutes, until slightly softened. In a bowl, mix the flour with enough bouillon to make a smooth paste and stir it into the pan. Cook, stirring, for 2 minutes, then gradually stir in the remaining bouillon. Add the bay leaf and season with salt and pepper. Bring to a boil, then lower the heat. Pour in the milk and wine, and stir in the lemon juice and grated zest. Simmer for 15 minutes.

Rinse the haddock under cold running water, then drain, and cut into bite-size chunks. Add them to the soup with the corn. Cook for 15 minutes, until the fish is tender and cooked through. Stir in the shrimp and the cream. Cook for another 2–3 minutes, then remove from the heat and discard the bay leaf.

Ladle into serving bowls, garnish with whole cooked shrimp, and serve with fresh whole-wheat bread and fresh salad greens.

mixed fish soup

		ingredients	
very easy	1 tbsp butter	10½ oz/300 g cod fillets, skinned
	2 shallots, chopped	7 oz/200 g canned or freshly
	1 leek, trimmed and sliced	cooked crabmeat
serves 4	3 tbsp all-purpose flour	5½ oz/150 g canned corn
	generous 2 cups fish bouillon	kernels, drained
	1 bay leaf	generous ¾ cup heavy cream
20 minutes	salt and pepper	
	generous 2 cups milk	TO GARNISH
	2 tbsp dry sherry	sprigs of fresh dill
40 minutes	2 tbsp lemon juice	wedges of lemon
	10½ oz/300 g haddock fillets, skinned	fresh crusty rolls, to serve

Melt the butter in a large pan over medium heat. Add the
shallots and leek and cook, stirring, for about 3 minutes, until
slightly softened. In a bowl, mix the flour with enough bouillon to
make a smooth paste, then stir it into the pan. Cook, stirring, for
2 minutes, then gradually stir in the remaining bouillon. Add the
bay leaf and season with salt and pepper. Bring to a boil, then
lower the heat. Pour in the milk and sherry, and stir in the lemon
juice. Simmer for 15 minutes.

Rinse the haddock and cod under cold running water, then drain
and cut into bite-size chunks. Add to the soup with the crabmeat
and corn. Cook for 15 minutes, until the fish is tender and cooked
through. Stir in the cream. Cook for another 2–3 minutes, then
remove from the heat and discard the bay leaf.

Ladle into serving bowls, garnish with sprigs of fresh dill and
lemon wedges, and serve with fresh crusty rolls.

bouillabaisse

		ingredients	
easy			
	scant ½ cup olive oil	7 oz/200 g live mussels	
	3 garlic cloves, chopped	9 oz/250 g snapper or monkfish fillets	
serves 4	2 onions, chopped	9 oz/250 g haddock fillets, skinned	
	2 tomatoes, seeded and chopped	7 oz/200 g shrimp, peeled and	
	generous 2¾ cups fish bouillon	deveined	
20 minutes +	1¾ cups white wine	3½ oz/100 g scallops	
10 minutes	1 bay leaf	salt and pepper	
to soak	pinch of saffron threads		
	2 tbsp chopped fresh basil	fresh baguettes, to serve	
45 minutes	2 tbsp chopped fresh parsley		

Heat the oil in a large pan over medium heat. Add the garlic and
onions and cook, stirring, for 3 minutes. Stir in the tomatoes,
bouillon, wine, bay leaf, saffron, and herbs. Bring to a boil, reduce
the heat, cover, and simmer for 30 minutes. Meanwhile, soak the
mussels in lightly salted water for 10 minutes. Scrub the shells
under cold running water and pull off any beards. Discard any with
broken shells. Tap the remaining mussels and discard any that
refuse to close. Put the rest into a large pan with a little water,
bring to a boil and cook over high heat for 4 minutes. Remove
from the heat and discard any that remain closed.

When the tomato mixture is cooked, rinse the fish, pat dry, and cut
into chunks. Add to the pan and simmer for 5 minutes. Add the
mussels, shrimp, and scallops, and season. Cook for 3 minutes,
until the fish is cooked through. Remove from the heat, discard the
bay leaf, and ladle into serving bowls. Serve with fresh baguettes.

seafood soup

		ingredients	
easy	2 lb 4 oz/1kg live mussels	1$\frac{1}{4}$ cups heavy cream
	$\frac{2}{3}$ cup dry white wine	1 tbsp cornstarch
serves 4	2 tbsp butter	7 oz/200 g shrimp, peeled
	1 onion, sliced	and deveined
	1 leek, trimmed and sliced	3$\frac{1}{2}$ oz/100 g scallops
15 minutes + 10 minutes to soak	3$\frac{1}{2}$ cups water	salt and pepper
	pinch of saffron threads	
	9 oz/250 g snapper fillets, skinned	sprigs of fresh dill, to garnish
35 minutes	9 oz/250 g haddock fillets, skinned	fresh whole-wheat rolls, to serve

Soak the mussels in salted water for 10 minutes. Scrub under cold running water; pull off any beards. Discard any with broken shells and any that refuse to close when tapped. Put the rest into a pan with the wine; bring to a boil. Cook over high heat for 4 minutes. Discard any that remain closed. Let cool. Lift out the mussels and remove the shells. Strain the cooking liquid and reserve. Melt the butter in a pan over medium heat. Add the onion and leek. Cook, stirring, for 3 minutes. Stir in the water, saffron, and cooking liquid. Bring to a boil, lower the heat, and simmer for 15 minutes.

Rinse the fish fillets, pat dry, and cut into small chunks. Add to the pan and simmer for 5 minutes. Stir in the cream. Blend the cornstarch in 2 tablespoons of water and stir into the soup. Add the shrimp and scallops, season, and cook for 2 minutes. Add the mussels and cook for 1 minute. Remove from the heat and ladle into serving bowls. Garnish the soup with sprigs of dill and serve with fresh whole-wheat rolls.

crab & vegetable soup

		ingredients	
	very easy	2 tbsp chili oil	1 tbsp grated lime zest
		1 garlic clove, chopped	6 kaffir lime leaves, finely shredded
		4 scallions, trimmed and sliced	10 1/2 oz/300 g freshly cooked crabmeat
	serves 4	2 red bell peppers, seeded	7 oz/200 g freshly cooked crab claws
		and chopped	5 1/2 oz/150 g canned corn
		1 tbsp grated fresh gingerroot	kernels, drained
	15–20	4 cups fish bouillon	2 tbsp chopped fresh cilantro
	minutes	salt and pepper	
		scant 1/2 cup coconut milk	TO GARNISH
		scant 1/2 cup rice wine or sherry	chopped fresh cilantro
	40 minutes	2 tbsp lime juice	thin strips of lime zest

Heat the oil in a large pan over medium heat. Add the garlic and scallions and cook, stirring, for about 3 minutes, until slightly softened. Add the bell peppers and gingerroot and cook for another 4 minutes, stirring. Pour in the bouillon and season with salt and pepper. Bring to a boil, then lower the heat. Pour in the coconut milk, rice wine, and lime juice, and stir in the grated lime zest and kaffir lime leaves. Simmer for 15 minutes.

Add the crabmeat and crab claws to the soup with the corn and cilantro. Cook the soup for 15 minutes, until the fish is tender and cooked right through.

Remove from the heat and ladle into serving bowls. Garnish with chopped fresh cilantro and strips of lime zest and serve.

spicy won ton soup

		ingredients	
	easy	2 garlic cloves, chopped	SOUP
		2 scallions, trimmed and chopped	1 tbsp chili oil or sesame oil
	serves 4	2 tsp light soy sauce	3 scallions, trimmed and sliced
		2 tsp sherry	1 small red chile, seeded and
		2 tbsp chopped fresh cilantro	finely chopped
		2 egg whites	1 red bell pepper, seeded and chopped
	20 minutes	3½ oz/100 g cooked shrimp, peeled	4 cups fish bouillon
		and chopped	1 tbsp light soy sauce
		3½ oz/100 g cooked chicken	2 tbsp sherry
	25 minutes	meat, chopped	1 tbsp chopped fresh cilantro
		16 won ton wrappers	1 tbsp chopped fresh parsley

To make the won tons, put the garlic, scallions, soy sauce, sherry, cilantro, and 1 egg white into a large bowl and mix well. Divide the mixture between 2 smaller bowls, then add the shrimp to one bowl and the chicken to the other. Spoon some shrimp mixture into the centers of 8 won ton wrappers, brush around the edges with the remaining egg white, then fold over into triangles and seal well. Take the 2 farthest corners of each triangle and join with egg white. Repeat the process with the remaining 8 won ton wrappers, this time using the chicken mixture.

To make the soup, heat the oil in a large skillet over medium heat. Add the scallions and cook, stirring, for 3 minutes. Add the chile and pepper and cook, stirring, for 5 minutes. Pour in the bouillon, soy sauce, sherry, and herbs. Bring to a boil, lower the heat, and simmer for 10 minutes. Add the won tons. Cook for 5–6 minutes. Remove from the heat, ladle into serving bowls, and serve hot.

shrimp & vegetable bisque

		ingredients	
	very easy	3 tbsp butter	salt and pepper
		1 garlic clove, chopped	1 lb 5 oz/600 g shrimp, peeled
	serves 4	1 onion, sliced	and deveined
		1 carrot, peeled and chopped	scant ½ cup heavy cream
		1 celery stalk, trimmed and sliced	
	15 minutes	5 cups fish bouillon	GARNISH
	+ 10 minutes	4 tbsp red wine	swirls of light cream
	to cool	1 tbsp tomato paste	whole cooked shrimp
		1 bay leaf	
	35 minutes		

Melt the butter in a large pan over medium heat. Add the garlic and onion and cook, stirring, for 3 minutes, until slightly softened. Add the carrot and celery and cook for another 3 minutes, stirring. Pour in the bouillon and red wine, then add the tomato paste and bay leaf. Season with salt and pepper. Bring to a boil, then lower the heat and simmer for 20 minutes. Remove from the heat and let cool for 10 minutes, then remove and discard the bay leaf.

Transfer half of the soup into a food processor and blend until smooth (you may need to do this in batches). Return to the pan with the rest of the soup. Add the shrimp and cook the soup over low heat for 5–6 minutes.

Stir in the cream and cook for another 2 minutes, then remove from the heat and ladle into serving bowls. Garnish with swirls of light cream and whole cooked shrimp, and serve at once.

poultry &
meat soups

The recipes in this section draw on a wide variety of ingredients and dishes from around the world, such as Scotch Broth and Indian Mulligatawny. There is also a Continental-style Salami & Vegetable Chowder, and a Pork & Vegetable Broth bursting with delicious Thai flavors. And for the cost-conscious among you, the Turkey & Lentil Soup provides an excellent way of using leftover turkey during the holidays or at other times during the year. You can also substitute leftover chicken for the turkey whenever the need arises.

chicken & potato soup
with bacon

		ingredients	
	very easy	1 tbsp butter	7 oz/200 g skinless chicken
		2 garlic cloves, chopped	breast, chopped
	serves 4	1 onion, sliced	salt and pepper
		9 oz/250 g smoked lean bacon,	4 tbsp heavy cream
		chopped	
		2 large leeks, trimmed and sliced	broiled bacon, chopped, to garnish
	15 minutes	2 tbsp all-purpose flour	
		4 cups chicken bouillon	fresh crusty rolls, to serve
		1 lb 12 oz/800 g potatoes, peeled	
	40 minutes	and chopped	

Melt the butter in a large pan over medium heat. Add the garlic
and onion and cook, stirring, for 3 minutes, until slightly softened.
Add the chopped bacon and leeks and cook for another 3 minutes,
stirring. In a bowl, mix the flour with enough bouillon to make a
smooth paste and stir it into the pan. Cook, stirring, for 2 minutes.
Pour in the remaining bouillon, then add the potatoes and chicken.
Season with salt and pepper. Bring to a boil, then lower the heat
and simmer for 25 minutes, until the chicken and potatoes are
tender and cooked through.

Stir in the cream and cook for another 2 minutes, then remove
from the heat and ladle into serving bowls. Garnish with chopped
bacon and serve with fresh crusty rolls.

cream of chicken soup

very easy	
serves 4	
15 minutes + 10 minutes to cool	
40 minutes	

ingredients

3 tbsp butter
4 shallots, chopped
1 leek, trimmed and sliced
1 lb/450 g skinless chicken
  breasts, chopped
2½ cups chicken bouillon
1 tbsp chopped fresh parsley

1 tbsp chopped fresh thyme
salt and pepper
¾ cup heavy cream

sprigs of fresh thyme, to garnish

fresh crusty rolls, to serve

Melt the butter in a large pan over medium heat. Add the shallots and cook, stirring, for 3 minutes, until slightly softened. Add the leek and cook for another 5 minutes, stirring. Add the chicken, bouillon, and herbs, and season with salt and pepper. Bring to a boil, then lower the heat and simmer for 25 minutes, until the chicken is tender and cooked through. Remove from the heat and let cool for 10 minutes.

Transfer the soup into a food processor and blend until smooth (you may need to do this in batches). Return the soup to the pan and warm over low heat for 5 minutes.

Stir in the cream and cook for another 2 minutes, then remove from the heat and ladle into serving bowls. Garnish with sprigs of thyme and serve with fresh crusty rolls.

turkey & lentil soup

		ingredients	
	very easy	1 tbsp olive oil	1 carrot, peeled and chopped
		1 garlic clove, chopped	1 cup red lentils
	serves 4	1 large onion, chopped	salt and pepper
		7 oz/200 g mushrooms, sliced	12 oz/350 g cooked turkey
		1 red bell pepper, seeded and chopped	meat, chopped
		6 tomatoes, skinned (see page 8),	1 zucchini, trimmed and chopped
	20 minutes	seeded, and chopped	1 tbsp shredded fresh basil
		generous 4 cups chicken bouillon	
		²/₃ cup red wine	fresh basil leaves, to garnish
	50 minutes	3 oz/85 g cauliflower florets	thick slices of fresh crusty bread,
			to serve

Heat the oil in a large pan. Add the garlic and onion and cook over medium heat, stirring, for 3 minutes, until slightly softened. Add the mushrooms, bell pepper, and tomatoes, and cook for another 5 minutes, stirring. Pour in the bouillon and red wine, then add the cauliflower, carrot, and red lentils. Season with salt and pepper. Bring to a boil, then lower the heat and simmer for 25 minutes, until the vegetables are tender and cooked through.

Add the turkey and zucchini to the pan and cook for 10 minutes. Stir in the shredded basil and cook for another 5 minutes, then remove from the heat and ladle into serving bowls. Garnish with fresh basil leaves and serve with slices of fresh crusty bread.

indian mulligatawny

very easy

serves 4

15–20
minutes

45 minutes

ingredients

2 tbsp vegetable oil
1 garlic clove, chopped
1 large onion, chopped
5½ oz/150 g mushrooms, sliced
2 tbsp all-purpose flour
4 cups chicken bouillon
7 oz/200 g skinless chicken
  breasts, chopped
5½ oz/150 g lean smoked
  ham, chopped
1 carrot, peeled and chopped

5½ oz/150 g potatoes, peeled
  and chopped
1 tbsp curry powder
salt and pepper
1 tbsp chopped fresh cilantro
½ cup heavy cream

GARNISH
grated fresh coconut
sprigs of fresh cilantro

fresh nan bread, to serve

Heat the oil in a large pan. Add the garlic and onion and cook over medium heat, stirring, for 3 minutes, until slightly softened. Add the mushrooms and cook for another 2 minutes. In a bowl, mix the flour with enough bouillon to make a smooth paste, then stir it into the pan. Stir in the remaining bouillon, then add the chicken, smoked ham, carrot, potatoes, and curry powder, and season with salt and pepper. Bring to a boil, then lower the heat and simmer very gently for 30 minutes until the meat and vegetables are tender and cooked through.

Stir in the cilantro and cream and cook for another 5 minutes. Remove from the heat and ladle into serving bowls. Garnish with grated coconut and sprigs of cilantro and serve with nan bread.

salami & vegetable chowder

		ingredients	
very easy	2 tbsp olive oil	5 $\frac{1}{2}$ oz/150 g white cabbage, chopped	
	1 garlic clove, chopped	1 zucchini, peeled and chopped	
	1 large onion, chopped	2 $\frac{3}{4}$ oz/75 g salami, sliced	
serves 4	2 tbsp all-purpose flour	$\frac{1}{2}$ cup heavy cream	
	4 cups vegetable bouillon		
	1 lb/450 g potatoes, peeled and sliced	fresh crusty rolls, to serve	
15 minutes	salt and pepper		
45 minutes			

Heat the oil in a large pan. Add the garlic and onion and cook over medium heat, stirring, for 3 minutes, until slightly softened. In a bowl, mix the flour with enough bouillon to make a smooth paste, then stir it into the pan. Stir in the remaining bouillon, then add the potatoes and season with salt and pepper. Bring to a boil, then lower the heat and simmer for 25 minutes, until the vegetables are tender and cooked through.

Add the cabbage, zucchini, and salami and cook for 10 minutes. Stir in the cream and cook for another 5 minutes. Remove from the heat, ladle into serving bowls and serve with fresh crusty rolls.

beef & cauliflower soup

		ingredients	
very easy		2 tbsp chili oil	salt and pepper
		1 garlic clove, chopped	9 oz/250 g lean beef, sliced
serves 4		3 scallions, trimmed and sliced	5½ oz/150 g cauliflower florets
		1 small red chile, seeded and	4½ oz/125 g broccoli florets
		finely chopped	
		1 red bell pepper, seeded and chopped	TO SERVE
15–20 minutes		4 cups beef bouillon	fresh salad greens
		1 tbsp soy sauce	fresh baguette
		2 tbsp rice wine or dry sherry	
40 minutes		5½ oz/150 g potatoes, peeled	
		and chopped	

Heat the oil in a large pan. Add the garlic, scallions, and chile and cook over medium heat, stirring, for 3 minutes, until slightly softened. Add the bell pepper and cook for 5 minutes, stirring. Pour in the bouillon, soy sauce, and rice wine, then add the potatoes and season with salt and pepper. Bring to a boil, then lower the heat and simmer for 15 minutes.

Add the beef, cauliflower, and broccoli and cook for another 15 minutes. Remove from the heat and ladle into serving bowls. Serve with fresh salad greens and fresh baguette.

cheese & bacon soup

		ingredients	
very easy		2 tbsp butter	salt and pepper
		2 garlic cloves, chopped	scant ½ cup heavy cream
serves 4		1 large onion, sliced	3 cups grated colby cheese
		9 oz/250 g smoked lean bacon, chopped	grated colby cheese, to garnish
15 minutes		2 large leeks, trimmed and sliced	fresh garlic bread, to serve
		2 tbsp all-purpose flour	
		4 cups vegetable bouillon	
40 minutes		1 lb/450 g potatoes, peeled and chopped	

Melt the butter in a large pan over medium heat. Add the garlic and onion and cook, stirring, for 3 minutes, until slightly softened. Add the chopped bacon and leeks and cook for another 3 minutes, stirring. In a bowl, mix the flour with enough bouillon to make a smooth paste and stir it into the pan. Cook, stirring, for 2 minutes. Pour in the remaining bouillon, then add the potatoes. Season with salt and pepper. Bring the soup to a boil, then lower the heat and simmer gently for 25 minutes, until the potatoes are tender and cooked through.

Stir in the cream and cook for 5 minutes, then gradually stir in the cheese until melted. Remove from the heat and ladle into individual serving bowls. Garnish with grated colby cheese and serve with fresh garlic bread.

pork & vegetable broth

		ingredients	
very easy	1 tbsp chili oil	1 small red chile, seeded and
	1 garlic clove, chopped	finely chopped
	3 scallions, trimmed and sliced	1 tbsp grated fresh gingerroot
serves 4	1 red bell pepper, seeded and	salt and pepper
	finely sliced	4 oz/115 g fine egg noodles
	2 tbsp cornstarch	7 oz/200 g canned water chestnuts,
15 minutes	4 cups vegetable bouillon	drained and sliced
	1 tbsp soy sauce	
	2 tbsp rice wine or dry sherry	TO SERVE
	5½ oz/150 g pork tenderloin, sliced	fresh salad greens
45 minutes	1 tbsp finely grated lemongrass	fresh crusty bread

Heat the oil in a large pan. Add the garlic and scallions and cook over medium heat, stirring, for 3 minutes, until slightly softened. Add the bell pepper and cook for another 5 minutes, stirring. In a bowl, mix the cornstarch with enough of the bouillon to make a smooth paste and stir it into the pan. Cook, stirring, for 2 minutes. Stir in the remaining bouillon and the soy sauce and rice wine, then add the pork, lemongrass, chile, and gingerroot. Season with salt and pepper. Bring to a boil, then lower the heat and simmer for 25 minutes.

Bring a separate pan of water to a boil, add the noodles, and cook for 3 minutes. Remove from the heat, drain, then add the noodles to the soup along with the water chestnuts. Cook for another 2 minutes, then remove from the heat and ladle into serving bowls. Serve with fresh salad greens and crusty bread.

sausage & red cabbage soup

		ingredients	
	very easy	2 tbsp olive oil	salt and pepper
		1 garlic clove, chopped	5½ oz/150 g red cabbage, chopped
	serves 4	1 large onion, chopped	7 oz/200 g canned black-eye
		1 large leek, trimmed and sliced	peas, drained
		2 tbsp cornstarch	½ cup heavy cream
	15 minutes	4 cups vegetable bouillon	ground paprika, to garnish
		1 lb/450 g potatoes, peeled and sliced	
		7 oz/200 g skinless sausages, sliced	fresh crusty rolls, to serve
	50 minutes		

Heat the oil in a large pan. Add the garlic and onion and cook over medium heat, stirring, for 3 minutes, until slightly softened. Add the leek and cook for another 3 minutes, stirring. In a bowl, mix the cornstarch with enough bouillon to make a smooth paste, then stir it into the pan. Cook, stirring, for 2 minutes. Stir in the remaining bouillon, then add the potatoes and sausages. Season with salt and pepper. Bring to a boil, then lower the heat and simmer for 25 minutes.

Add the red cabbage and black-eye peas and cook for 10 minutes, then stir in the cream and cook for another 5 minutes. Remove from the heat and ladle into serving bowls. Garnish with ground paprika and serve with fresh crusty rolls.

scotch broth

		ingredients	
very easy		2¾ oz/75 g pearl barley, rinsed and drained	9 oz/250 g potatoes, peeled and sliced
		1 tbsp vegetable oil	1 large carrot, peeled and chopped
serves 4		1 garlic clove, chopped	5½ oz/150 g rutabaga, peeled and chopped
		1 large onion, chopped	1 turnip, peeled and chopped
		1 large leek, trimmed and sliced	2 celery stalks, trimmed and sliced
20 minutes		generous 4 cups vegetable bouillon	2 tsp dried mixed herbs
		1 bay leaf	
		1 lb/450 g lean boneless lamb, fat	sprigs of fresh parsley, to garnish
1½ hours		trimmed away	slices of fresh whole-wheat bread,
		salt and pepper	to serve

Bring a pan of water to a boil. Add the barley and boil over high heat for 5 minutes, skimming the surface when necessary. Remove from the heat and set aside.

Heat the oil in a large pan. Add the garlic and onion and cook over medium heat, stirring, for 3 minutes, until slightly softened. Add the leek and cook for another 4 minutes, stirring. Stir in the bouillon, then drain the barley and add to the pan along with the bay leaf. Cut the lamb into bite-size chunks and add to the pan. Season with salt and pepper. Bring to a boil, then lower the heat and simmer for 15 minutes. Add the potatoes, carrot, rutabaga, turnip, celery, and mixed herbs and cook for 1 hour.

Remove from the heat, discard the bay leaf, and ladle into serving bowls. Garnish the Scotch broth with sprigs of fresh parsley and serve with slices of fresh whole-wheat bread.

beans, grains & noodles

Comforting soups containing beans, grains, and noodles are heartwarming at any time of the year. Many of the recipes in this section use canned beans because they are convenient, but you can use dried if you prefer. Simply adjust the soaking and cooking times accordingly. The times vary according to the type of bean, so always check the instructions on the package. Whether you use canned or dried beans, these soups are highly nutritious, and many need only fresh crusty bread to transform them into satisfying meals in themselves.

spicy lentil soup

		ingredients	
	very easy	1 tbsp olive oil	1 tbsp chopped fresh parsley
		1 onion, sliced	pinch of saffron threads
	serves 4	1 leek, trimmed and sliced	1 tsp ground coriander
		scant 5½ cups vegetable bouillon	1 tsp garam masala
		1 carrot, peeled and chopped	salt and pepper
	10–15 minutes	1 celery stalk, trimmed and sliced	sprigs of fresh cilantro, to garnish
		generous ⅓ cup brown rice	
		1 cup red lentils	fresh whole-wheat bread, to serve
		1 bay leaf	
	50 minutes		

Heat the oil in a large pan. Add the onion and cook over medium heat, stirring, for 3 minutes, until slightly softened. Add the leek and cook for another 2 minutes, stirring. Stir in the bouillon, then add the carrot, celery, rice, lentils, herbs, and spices. Season with salt and pepper. Bring to a boil, then lower the heat and simmer for 40 minutes until the rice, lentils, and vegetables are tender and cooked through.

Remove the soup from the heat and discard the bay leaf. Ladle into serving bowls, garnish with sprigs of fresh cilantro, and serve with fresh whole-wheat bread.

pea & ham soup

		ingredients	
	very easy	1 tbsp butter	1 tbsp chopped fresh tarragon
		1 onion, sliced	salt and pepper
	serves 4	1 leek, trimmed and sliced	4 tbsp heavy cream
		4 cups vegetable bouillon	
		1 lb/450 g freshly shelled peas, or	GARNISH
	10–15 minutes + 10 minutes to cool	frozen peas, thawed	cooked ham, chopped
		7 oz/200 g lean smoked ham, chopped	sprigs of fresh tarragon
		1 bay leaf	
	45 minutes		fresh crusty rolls, to serve

Melt the butter in a large pan over medium heat. Add the onion and cook, stirring, for 3 minutes, until slightly softened. Add the leek and cook for another 2 minutes, stirring. Stir in the bouillon, then add the peas, ham, bay leaf, and tarragon. Season with salt and pepper. Bring to a boil, then lower the heat and simmer for 30 minutes. Remove from the heat and discard the bay leaf. Let cool for 10 minutes.

Transfer half of the soup into a food processor and blend until smooth. Return to the pan with the rest of the soup, stir in the cream, and cook over low heat for another 5 minutes.

Remove the soup from the heat and ladle into serving bowls. Garnish with chopped ham and sprigs of fresh tarragon and serve with fresh crusty rolls.

soupe au pistou

		ingredients	
	very easy	PISTOU SAUCE	1 lb/450 g potatoes, chopped
		scant 1 cup chopped fresh basil	3½ oz/100 g thin green beans
		scant ½ cup chopped fresh parsley	1 large carrot, peeled and chopped
	serves 4	3 garlic cloves, finely chopped	7 oz/200 g canned cannellini beans
		5 tbsp extra-virgin olive oil	5½ oz/150 g lean smoked ham, chopped
		3 tbsp freshly grated Parmesan	14 oz/400 g canned tomatoes
	25 minutes	FOR THE SOUP	1 tbsp chopped fresh thyme
		2 tbsp extra-virgin olive oil	salt and pepper
		1 garlic clove, finely chopped	2¾ oz/75 g dried vermicelli
	40 minutes	1 onion, chopped	shavings of fresh Parmesan, to garnish
		5 cups vegetable bouillon	slices of fresh bread, to serve

To make the pistou, put all the ingredients into a food processor and blend until combined. Transfer into a bowl, cover with plastic wrap, and chill.

To make the soup, heat the oil in a large pan over medium heat. Add the garlic and the onion and cook, stirring, for 3 minutes, until slightly softened. Stir in the bouillon, then add the potatoes, green beans (which have been topped and tailed, then finely chopped), carrot, drained cannellini beans, and ham, and the tomatoes with their juices. Stir in the thyme and season. Bring to a boil, then lower the heat and simmer for 20 minutes. Add the vermicelli and cook for another 12 minutes, or according to the instructions on the package.

Remove from the heat and ladle into serving bowls. Put a generous spoonful of pistou sauce into each bowl, garnish with fresh Parmesan shavings, and serve with slices of fresh bread.

mixed bean soup
with swiss cheese

	ingredients

very easy

serves 4

15 minutes + 10 minutes to cool

55 minutes

1 tbsp extra-virgin olive oil
3 garlic cloves, finely chopped
4 scallions, trimmed and sliced
7 oz/200 g mushrooms, sliced
4 cups vegetable bouillon
1 large carrot, peeled and chopped
14 oz/400 g canned mixed
   beans, drained
1 lb 12 oz/800 g canned
   chopped tomatoes

1 tbsp chopped fresh thyme
1 tbsp chopped fresh oregano
salt and pepper
6 oz/175 g Swiss cheese, grated
4 tbsp heavy cream

GARNISH
swirls of light cream
finely chopped scallions

thick slices of fresh bread, to serve

Heat the oil in a large pan over medium heat. Add the garlic and scallions and cook, stirring, for 3 minutes, until slightly softened. Add the mushrooms and cook for another 2 minutes, stirring. Stir in the bouillon, then add the carrot, mixed beans, chopped tomatoes, and herbs. Season with salt and pepper. Bring to a boil, then lower the heat and simmer for 30 minutes. Remove from the heat and let cool for 10 minutes.

Transfer into a food processor and blend until smooth. Return to the pan and stir in the cheese. Cook for another 10 minutes, then stir in the cream. Cook for 5 minutes, then remove from the heat and ladle into serving bowls. Garnish with swirls of cream and chopped or sliced scallions. Serve with thick slices of fresh bread.

sweet potato & lentil soup

		ingredients	
	very easy	1 tbsp olive oil	1 carrot, peeled and chopped
		1 garlic clove, chopped	1 cup red lentils
	serves 4	1 large onion, chopped	salt and pepper
		1 red bell pepper, seeded and chopped	1 tbsp chopped fresh basil
	15–20 minutes + 10 minutes to cool	6 tomatoes, skinned (see page 8), seeded and chopped	sprigs of fresh basil, to garnish
		4 cups vegetable bouillon	fresh crusty rolls, to serve
	55 minutes	1 lb/450 g sweet potatoes, peeled and chopped	

Heat the oil in a large pan. Add the garlic and onion and cook over medium heat, stirring, for 3 minutes, until slightly softened. Add the bell pepper and the tomatoes and cook for another 2 minutes, stirring. Pour in the bouillon, then add the sweet potatoes, carrot, and lentils. Season with salt and pepper. Bring to a boil, then lower the heat and simmer for 30 minutes, until all of the vegetables are tender and cooked through. Remove from the heat and let cool for 10 minutes.

Transfer half of the soup into a food processor and blend until smooth. Return to the pan with the rest of the soup and cook for 10 minutes. Stir in the chopped basil and cook for another 5 minutes. Remove from the heat and ladle into serving bowls. Garnish with sprigs of fresh basil and serve with fresh crusty rolls.

chorizo & red kidney bean soup

			ingredients	
very easy		2 tbsp olive oil	5 ½ oz/150 g chorizo, sliced	
		2 garlic cloves, chopped	2 zucchini, trimmed and sliced	
serves 4		2 red onions, chopped	7 oz/200 g canned red kidney	
		1 red bell pepper, seeded and chopped	beans, drained	
		2 tbsp cornstarch	½ cup heavy cream	
15–20 minutes		4 cups vegetable bouillon	slices of fresh crusty bread, to serve	
		1 lb/450 g potatoes, peeled, halved, and sliced		
		salt and pepper		
50 minutes				

Heat the oil in a large pan. Add the garlic and onions and cook over medium heat, stirring, for 3 minutes, until slightly softened. Add the bell pepper and cook for another 3 minutes, stirring. In a bowl, mix the cornstarch with enough bouillon to make a smooth paste and stir it into the pan. Cook, stirring, for 2 minutes. Stir in the remaining bouillon, then add the potatoes and season with salt and pepper. Bring to a boil, then lower the heat and simmer for 25 minutes, until the vegetables are tender.

Add the chorizo, zucchini, and kidney beans to the pan. Cook for 10 minutes, then stir in the cream and cook for another 5 minutes. Remove from the heat and ladle into serving bowls. Serve with slices of fresh crusty bread.

tomato, rice & tarragon soup

		ingredients	
	very easy	2 tbsp olive oil	generous ¾ cup brown rice
		2 garlic cloves, chopped	1 tbsp chopped fresh tarragon
	serves 4	2 red onions, chopped	salt and pepper
		1 red bell pepper, seeded and chopped	scant ½ cup heavy cream
		8 tomatoes, skinned (see page 8), seeded and chopped	sprigs of fresh tarragon, to garnish
	20 minutes + 10 minutes to cool	4 cups vegetable bouillon	fresh crusty bread, to serve
		1 celery stalk, trimmed and sliced	
	50 minutes		

Heat the oil in a large pan. Add the garlic and onions and cook over medium heat, stirring, for 3 minutes, until slightly softened. Add the bell pepper and the tomatoes and cook for another 2 minutes, stirring. Stir in the bouillon, then add the celery, rice, and tarragon. Season with salt and pepper. Bring to a boil, then lower the heat and simmer for 30 minutes. Remove from the heat and let cool for 10 minutes.

Transfer half of the soup into a food processor and blend until smooth. Return to the pan with the rest of the soup and cook for 5 minutes. Stir in the cream and cook for another 5 minutes. Remove from the heat and ladle into serving bowls. Garnish with sprigs of fresh tarragon and serve with fresh crusty bread.

chicken, mushroom & barley soup

		ingredients	
very easy	2¾ oz/75 g pearl barley, rinsed and drained	9 oz/250 g crimini mushrooms, sliced
serves 4	2 tbsp butter 1 large onion, sliced 1 large leek, trimmed and sliced 4 cups chicken bouillon	1 large carrot, peeled and chopped 1 tbsp chopped fresh oregano 1 bay leaf sprigs of fresh flatleaf parsley, to garnish
15 minutes	salt and pepper 1 lb/450 g skinless chicken breasts, chopped	fresh crusty bread, to serve
1½ hours		

Bring a pan of water to a boil. Add the barley and boil over high heat for 5 minutes, skimming the surface when necessary. Remove from the heat and set aside.

Melt the butter in a large pan. Add the onion and cook over medium heat, stirring, for 3 minutes, until slightly softened. Add the leek and cook for another 4 minutes, stirring. Stir in the bouillon, then drain the barley and add to the pan. Season with salt and pepper. Bring to a boil, then lower the heat and simmer for 45 minutes. Add the chicken, mushrooms, carrot, oregano, and bay leaf. Cook for another 30 minutes.

Remove from the heat and discard the bay leaf. Ladle into serving bowls, garnish with sprigs of fresh flatleaf parsley, and serve with fresh crusty bread.

minestrone

		ingredients	
very easy	2 tbsp olive oil	14 oz/400 g canned borlotti
	2 garlic cloves, chopped	beans, drained
serves 4	2 red onions, chopped	3 1/2 oz/100 g green leafy
	2 3/4 oz/75 g prosciutto, sliced	cabbage, shredded
	1 red bell pepper, seeded and chopped	2 3/4 oz/75 g frozen peas, thawed
15–20 minutes	1 orange bell pepper, seeded and chopped	1 tbsp chopped fresh parsley
	14 oz/400 g canned chopped tomatoes	salt and pepper
	4 cups vegetable bouillon	2 3/4 oz/75 g dried vermicelli
45–50 minutes	1 celery stalk, trimmed and sliced	freshly grated Parmesan cheese, to garnish
		fresh crusty bread, to serve

Heat the oil in a large pan. Add the garlic, onions, and prosciutto and cook over medium heat, stirring, for 3 minutes, until slightly softened. Add the red and orange bell peppers and the chopped tomatoes and cook for another 2 minutes, stirring. Stir in the bouillon, then add the celery, borlotti beans, cabbage, peas, and parsley. Season with salt and pepper. Bring to a boil, then lower the heat and simmer for 30 minutes.

Add the vermicelli to the pan. Cook for another 10–12 minutes, or according to the instructions on the package. Remove from the heat and ladle into serving bowls. Garnish with freshly grated Parmesan and serve with fresh crusty bread.

bean curd & noodle broth

		ingredients	
very easy		1 tbsp sesame oil	4 cups vegetable bouillon
		1 garlic clove, chopped	2¾ oz/75 g dried fine egg noodles
serves 4		4 scallions, trimmed and sliced	3½ oz/100 g firm bean curd, drained
		1 small red chile, seeded and	and cut into small cubes
		finely chopped	salt and pepper
15 minutes		1¾ oz/50 g shiitake mushrooms, sliced	
		1¾ oz/50 g crimini mushrooms, sliced	chopped fresh cilantro, to garnish
		1 tbsp rice wine	fresh crusty bread, to serve
5 minutes		2 tsp soy sauce	
		2 tbsp chopped fresh cilantro	

Heat the oil in a large wok or pan over high heat. Add the garlic, scallions, and chile and stir-fry for 1 minute, until slightly softened. Add the mushrooms, rice wine, soy sauce, cilantro, and bouillon and bring to a boil. Lower the heat, add the noodles, and simmer the soup gently for 3 minutes.

Add the bean curd and season with salt and pepper. Remove from the heat, then transfer into individual serving bowls. Garnish with chopped fresh cilantro and serve with fresh crusty bread.

index